Oh, I Pretend

Poems by Pat Beckemeyer

Kansas City   Spartan Press   Missouri

Spartan Press
Kansas City, Missouri
spartanpresskc.com

Copyright © Pat Beckemeyer, 2019
First Edition 1 3 5 7 9 10 8 6 4 2
ISBN: 978-1-950380-73-2
LCCN: 2019954916

Design, edits and layout: Jason Ryberg
Cover image: Jon Lee Grafton
Title page image: Roy Beckemeyer
Author photo: Roy Beckemeyer
All rights reserved. No part of this publication may be reproduced or transmitted in any form or by any means, electronic or mechanical, including photocopying, recording or by info retrieval system, without prior written permission from the author.

Acknowledgments:

Thanks to Wayward Poets for their help and inspiration the past 10 years, to Basement Bards for the to-the-point critiquing, and for teaching me (almost) to be quiet during said critiquing, and to ICT Poets at the Wichita Public Library for their help via critiques and classes. Melany Pearce and Dixie Brown read through the draft manuscript and suggested improvements.

"Field Sparrow" first appeared in *To the Stars through Difficulties: A Kansas Renga in 150 Voices* (2013, Caryn Mirriam-Goldberg, Mammoth Publications, Lawrence, KS). "Fair-Haired Girl," "Family," "Oh, I Pretend," and "Rifles," all first appeared in *River City Poetry*, Fall Issue, 2018. "Rain at the Golf Course" won 2nd Place, Narrative Poetry, in the 2016 Kansas Authors Club Poetry Contest. The haiku, "whispering breeze," won 1st place, Japanese Forms, in the 2016 Kansas Authors Club Poetry Contest. "Xenophobic Alphabet" won 2nd Place, Whimsy, in the 2016 Kansas Authors Club Poetry Contest.

Table of Contents

To Have Pain Is to Feel

Family / 1
Cessation / 3
Freedom / 4
Xenophobic Alphabet / 5
Homeless / 6
Dementia's Alphabet / 7
Memories / 9
Bogeyman in the Dark / 10
A Man Is Gone / 12
I Told Him / 13
Back When / 14
Reunion / 15

She Swirls Under Starlight

Rifles / 19
Spring Sprouts / 20
Walk with Spring / 21
Mournful Cries / 22
Missing / 23
whispering breezes / 24
Tattered / 25
sitting in the sun / 26
Big Blue Butterflies / 27
Field Sparrow / 28

I'm a Young Dog

Rain at the Golf Course / 31
Fair-Haired Girl / 32
drifting / 33
Fairytale / 34
Lemon Moon / 35
The Fire Within / 36
Walking the Dog / 37
Will the Chickens Come Home to Roost? / 38
warm waters / 40
My Wish for Us / 41
Rising / 42

Oh, I Pretend!

Oh, I Pretend / 45
his voice / 46
Silently Sliding / 48
Sam / 49
You Are Mine / 50
My Love / 51
When I Die / 52
The Circle / 53

To Roy, my love forever, for incentive, inspiration, and patience.

To Have Pain Is to Feel

Family

My family was like a jar of grasshoppers.
We fed on each other.
We ate each other alive.
We wanted out.

It was not butterflies we wanted to be.
Not anything that beautiful.
Not anything that free.
We just wanted out.

We were like a nest of wasps.
Wanting to sting you, repeatedly.
Until you died screaming.
We fed on pain.

Hurtful, Hateful, Horrendous.
Speaking was meant to draw blood.
To make it flow freely, forever, fatally.
To have pain is to feel.

We were like cicadas, screeching at night.
Empty shells of selves littered our tree.
We thought this would free us,
But hornets ate us at our birth.

Repeatedly trying to emerge,
We became trapped forever crumbling.
Seeing no way free from our tree,
We wailed like sirens in the night.

Cessation

Mindless as a stone,
I sit staring out the window.
The continuum of space and time
races by, but like a stone,
my mind does not move
of its own volition.

Thinking only evokes
the sadness of the emptiness
that is my life.
My friends have left me,
one by one, as I drove them off.

Food no longer nourishes
the emptiness within my bowels.
Nor does air fill the hollowness
within my empty soul.

I bear no wish to continue.
This, I will end.

Freedom

dancing sadly naked
eyes diverted from
gratuitous gazes of
gawking strangers

once proud tribesmen
expose their bodies
trying to tell themselves
it no longer matters

Xenophobic Alphabet

Always
believe
chauvinism
decides
experience
for
genocidal
humans.

Irrational
jingoistic
killing
leaves
men
numb
over
periodic
quarrelsome
rioting.

Selective
thinking
urges
vague
wisdomless
xenophobic
yelling
zealots.

Homeless

Standing on the corner
homeless men huddled together
with staring blank eyes
apparently seeing naught.

Their bodies pressed together
closely enough to deny entry
to the howling winds of winter.

One man stood alone
he looked like half a leaf
as if the first strong wind
would carry him to his grave.

Dementia's Alphabet

Always having been considered bright,
being ever at the head of the class,
can you imagine my devastation,
declaring *I don't remember who you are?*

Everybody forgets words at times.
Fortunately, someone is always glad to help.
Getting stopped dead in the middle of my story,
having no idea what I have said,

I flounder around and declare, *It was
just not that important anyway.*
Knowing, as you do, that I
lose it a lot lately, I think that

maybe you can feel my mind slipping,
never to be hoisted high again.
Only for you, it's not a personal insult,
perhaps only a bad moment in your day.

Quaking with fear, wondering what
racking indignity will next befall,
sometimes I simply long to escape,
trying not to think of the future.

Unless you, too, have lost something as
valuable as your mind and memories,
withhold any impulse to say you understand,
x-ing out my right to mourn the future.

You will soon go your way, and I mine,
zealously waiting for that elusive cure.

Memories

Compared to some folks I am a genius,
but others exist to whom I cannot speak.

Peeling layers off my memory makes me
see that what I was is not what I am now.

Like others before me, words now escape.
Knowledge has been tainted by the years.

Faces I know as well as my own,
stand beside me with no name.

Blank years of my life now exist,
for I do not remember my own children.

No hope exists to find these memories,
for those who knew are gone from time.

Hunger for the past I've foolishly lost
strains my mind to seek where it hides.

Exactly as I left it, does not describe
scenes from the past, alive in my mind.

Across the many years of time,
memories are not what they seem.

So leave me alone now.
I can still dream.

Bogeyman in the Dark

Thinking,
remembering,
forgetting,
trying to forget.

The poignancy of the moment
won't be forgotten—
it's always there,
waiting to sneak
into each new memory,
saying *Don't forget me—
I won't be forgotten.*

I'm forging a new life now,
happier days than those
I'm trying to forget.
But those old memories
won't go away, they hide,
popping up to surprise me
when I least expect.

Day by day I'll forge
new memories, forcing out
the old until they have no room
to pop back in unexpectedly,

until they are dragged away
kicking and screaming
by those bogeymen in the dark
that I know so well.

A Man Is Gone

A man is gone
My son
The loss is too great to bear
I will not pick it up
I will not carry it
For then I should have to claim it
And it would be
Too real
Too heavy
Too much
I will not claim it
But it is mine

I Told Him

I told him it was okay
he could go now
he could give up this painful
dying state

I told him our
life together
had been so wonderful
that the memories of the years
would hold me together

I told him
I would be okay

I lied

—*Inspired by Linda Rondstadt's "Goodbye My Friend"*

Back When

Our feelings were worn on silvered sleeves.
While our hearts heaved silently stillborn.

Labors of love lasted us a lifetime,
But love itself carried not the course.

End of life beckoned us to bravely come,
Though the beginning held us enthralled.

In God We Trust was our father's faith,
Yet our trust was tumultuously shaken.

Death we wish would beckon us to it,
But life digs in her claws to shred our skin.

We sometimes crave attention too much,
Yet shrink unbidden under her stare.

Greet all as if they were family friends,
While keeping track of their wrongs and faults.

Never silence those who speak well of you,
But listen carefully to their choice of words.

Bring the world closer and push it away.

Reunion

The end of my journey is in sight.
Rounding the corner, I see my home.

Headlights highlight the house,
flickering like lightning bugs gone mad.

Chasing my tail has come to this end,
that which I ran from and returned to,

a memory, a memoir of my life,
now no longer exists.

Dark days of my childhood are over;
I am no one's child, for mother is gone.

Across the porch a gurney comes;
The face for which I returned is lost.

Sometimes this was what I wished for.
Sometimes I wanted to be held again.

Birch colored limbs are uncovered.
The face of a pale moon lies wan.

She Swirls Under Starlight

Rifles

Walking in the open, frozen field,
Freed for the night from driven golfers,
My dog running frenetically beside me,
Frantic to keep her feet unfrozen,
Running like a yearling deer,
She leaps and swirls under starlight.

Sounds like rifle shots signal danger.
She stops in mid-leap landing solid.
What are these snapping sniper sounds
Mysteriously magnified in frozen stillness?
Suddenly I halt to somehow find
What danger exists to the dog and me.

Tree trunks around me are splitting,
Some down the middle as if axed.
Other limbs are smaller, but bigger
than a man hewn in the prime of life.
Falling ice is taking them down.
It is in frozen water that they drown.

Spring Sprouts

I picked today to walk in the woods.
Last night's rain, falling softly and silently,

was the catalyst for green spring sprouts
petulantly pushing their noses above the earth,

enjoying their first warm whiff of air,
simultaneously sending oxygen to their roots,

everything was now perfectly primed
for verdant carpet coverage of

the floor by fallen leaves.
Violets, now through with vanity,

rain soaking their roots, were ready
to yield ground to greener grass.

The smell of fresh growth
ignited the illusion of eternity.

Paths, fighting frantically for survival,
beckoned boots to wander through spring.

Walk with Spring

and my dog, of course.
We walk slowly.
She is sniffing the ground,
I am inhaling the smell
of wisteria, roses, viburnum.

She is enthralled with squirrels.
I am entranced with
daffodils opening, smiling,
trumpet daffodils
blaring the news of rebirth.

She sniffs the air thoughtfully.
What nuances can she smell?
Right now, I'm into colors.
Look how cleverly the larkspurs
accentuate the yellows of daffodils.

She is listening now, ears pricked.
Can she hear plants emerging?
I hear the song of the robin.
I think I hear the tree grow.
Spring has enhanced me.

Mournful Cries

Above our heads, the mournful cry of the owl
echoes like a spirit crying in the twilight.

He's as big as a large cat perched in the tree,
with eyes like round golden reflectors.
Having movement like a surveillance camera,
they follow us, but the body is still.

Then, silently, no sound of wings, no voice,
a looming specter floats over our heads,

suddenly making a nosedive through
a shelter of dead leaves under the old oak.

A rabbit screams, then returns quietly
with the owl to his perch, sates his hunger.

Missing

feeder taken down
birds missing
sweet call of chickadee
unheard

goldfinches
changing to bright color
somewhere else
not here

eerie sweet call
of Harris sparrow
in bushes
someone else's

when old age
limits gardening
not just the flowers
are missing

whispering breezes

whispering breezes
   tell tales of forests long gone
dying trees listen

Tattered

she settled on the purple flower
her wings had seen better days
tattered and broken, she could still fly

she did not know that some
saw her as less than beautiful
and she did not care

nectar still tasted like proverbial manna
the gentle breeze still lifted her wings
her soul was yet a beautiful butterfly
her butterfly spirit yet sings

sitting in the sun

chaise lounge with its feet in the grass
facing just right
so the sun doesn't shine in my eyes

warmth caresses me
and seeps into my marrow
warming within and without

cold glass of iced tea perches on table
digging its toes in so it doesn't fall
ice melting like the icebergs

dog and cat down-side up
soaking sun through already warm bellies
moaning softly to the grass

I feel my body softening, melting
becoming one with
the heat of the sun

Big Blue Butterflies

they were there
the big blue butterflies
I had sought
across continents

Morphos glued to paper
spread out on pages
small, medium, or large
symmetrical or scattered
 trivial and trite

but living Morphos
slow, rhythmic, wingbeats
Byzantine blue,
slow flying
in a cloud forest,
living beauty untouched,
are seared forever
in my mind

Field Sparrow

Did you ever hear a field sparrow sing
her ethereal, piercing, heart-rending notes?
After you follow the sound to its source
you expect to find an angel, or maybe a fairy.

But as you arrive at the source of the song
you find a nondescript little brown sparrow,
joy from her being escaping with each trill.

Perhaps our notion of what an angel looks like
has been guided falsely by Renaissance pictures.
Perhaps she is sitting here singing in a little brown coat.

I'm a Young Dog

Rain at the Golf Course

Inspired by "Rain in the Park," by Lisa Silverberg

My dog and I
are playing
like frantic children
running through puddles
digging holes in sand
lying on grass
washed by rain

Don't tell anyone
I'm an old woman
least of all me
I'm a child again
not caring
who sees
I'm a young dog
playing wild again

Fair-Haired Girl

I longed to be the fair-haired girl
straight blond hair to her shoulders
flipping and swirling as she turned her head
perfect figure pirouetting through time
as she was thrown into the air
landing softly like a sparrow on a branch

my fate was to have unruly brown hair
a body that couldn't balance to flip
longing for what I couldn't have
nevertheless I swirled through time
shining like a star without a moon
twinkling as a beacon so all could see
what they really wanted was a girl like me

drifting

each drifts alone through life
someone may drift beside us
but ultimately, we are alone,
alone to face the end or the music

slowly move along your way
so you may stop or veer as needed
should another be drifting with you
hold on…your chances are better

eventually moons or comets
separate one from the other
galaxies collide, stars burn up,
no one will be there forever

drift so that if goodness prevails
you can hover there for awhile
if evil assails you prepare to
grab the tail of a comet

never trust stability
relationships change
moons become full
then break apart
drifting carefully is an art

Fairytale

How I long to see a cow
jump ever so quickly
across the moon.

The moon that's now shining
slathers of apricot syrup
across the face of my love.

Landscape now brightened
brings my garden alive,
trying to lure me to the path.

Fills me with memories of
fairies flittering from flower
to bush, fulfilling a hidden wish.

Figures of Cheshire cats
cuddling in covered corners,
complete this scene of disbelief.

Reality hits as the moon
goes behind a vagrant cloud,
carrying a satchel of flowers.

Gossip says that those who
love gardens will grow old
as wise as the Mad Hatter.

Lemon Moon

The moon looked
like an enormous
smiling lemon
who had taken a bite
of the earth.

A large bird flew back
and forth across my
view of the moon
swooning and calling
as if the moon had taken
its fledgling.

Here on my home street
sitting, rocking on my porch,
I wonder what other things,
what tragedies,
what wonders,
happen up there
beyond our life sustenance,
our air.

The Fire Within

Mindless like a stone,
I sit staring out the window.
Raindrops splatter their bodies
against the dust stained window,
then run like scared mice
back to ground.

Fingers of earth reach up,
grabbing raindrops by their throats,
pulling them down into their bowels,
to cool the fire within.

My mind drifts back,
wondering about the fire.

Walking the dog

together
we move linked as one
linked by leash
linked by love
joys of nature assail us
each in her own way

Will the Chickens Come Home to Roost?

Before I go back to square one, or vanish into thin air,
Or cook a different kettle of fish,
Or drink that proverbial drop in the ocean,
I really must find my missing chickens.

Birds of a feather are supposed to flock together.
And these chickens don't have their wings clipped.
So, I suppose when you get right down to it
The sky is the limit; they might be flying high.

I'm out in the pasture, making hay while the sun shines.
Visited my horse, Snicker, but since he's a gift,
Didn't look him in the mouth. Can't find my dogs again.
They are probably barking up the wrong tree somewhere.

But still waiting for the chickens to come home to roost.
I think soon they would come back, like a moth to the flame.
Guess while I'm out in the pasture, waiting for those chickens,
I could get those lambs and lead them to the slaughter.

My cats are gone too, I'm worried about them.
They are out stalking something, and curiosity killed the cat.
But here comes one now, grinning like a Cheshire cat.
I hope those darned cats haven't been eating chicken.

It's past time for breakfast, I've developed a deep hunger.
Since you can't make an omelet without breaking a few eggs,
I ventured out to get me at least a dozen of them,
but can't put your eggs all in one basket, with no chickens.

warm waters

dip gently
into warm waters
body flows
like fluid
painlessly I move about
like a young otter

My Wish for Us

I wish us jazz bands and bagpipes,
bird song, and sunsets.

I wish us sunrises, bull frogs, butterflies,
and battalions of flowers.

I wish us a moist dog tongue to sooth
all hurts, and a cat's purr to pace our hearts.

I wish us fireworks, Milky Ways,
and puppies to smell and kiss.

But most of all I wish us together,
in a world filled with bliss.

Rising

rising as in a dream
floating like a bubble
my spirit haunts the house

the dog stirs in her sleep
but does not smell me
for I have no odor
she does not hear me
for I make no sound
but she does feel my presence

she whimpers and
wraps her tail around her nose

Oh, I Pretend!

Oh, I Pretend!

I swim a lap back to the end
my legs feel peaceful when they bend
full length today I can extend
Oh, I pretend, Oh I pretend

but when I walk these legs offend
don't always do as I intend
in the water I can transcend
Oh, I pretend, Oh I pretend

his voice

I thought he was gone
but I hear his voice
I remember it
like yesterday
it resonates
within my heart

his face
coming around
the corner
blinds my eyes
I never expected
to see it again
my heart screams

my body and soul
tremble as one
my voice is silent
what should I say
to an apparition
a remembrance
the reincarnation
of my love, my one

you're here
I love you still
kiss me
hold me
let's be one again
forever.

Silently Sliding

Spreading my arms wide, I hope to clasp you inside.
You have filled this void many lifetimes.

Everywhere I go, I want you to be there with me.
When my heart beats alone, it has no pacer.

But my life goes on without your presence,
A sick and paltry version of itself with you.

Heading down this sad slippery slope,
I find no staff, no limb, to hold onto.

Mostly I slide singing silly songs and
Crying in time to the music of Mozart.

West is the direction my compass is pointing,
but East is where I might have gone with you.

Sam

You were the best. Sam.
Always there when I needed you.

As I stand by this stately elm,
gazing heartbroken, at your grave
Tears fall. Not all from sorrow.

Fourteen joyful years with you
Cemented our souls together.

We were quite different animals.
But somehow even in our difference,
Our friendship filled some primal need.

Now in separated togetherness
We will each go our own way
This time you lead, I will follow.

You Are Mine

You are my tapioca, smooth but with the right texture, melting against my tongue.

You are my hot buttered rum, savory and sweet, but with a kick.

You are my chickadee, soft voice, and strong wings to flee from harm.

You are my opal, your color, and those of your jewel tones, not named.

You are my weeping willow, graceful arms draped for protection, hiding your sturdiness within.

You are my maroon tulip bright and open in the morning but closed tightly at night to protect yourself while you sleep.

You are my ocean, coming in with swells, then slipping away.

You are my faithful Labrador, quiet by my side, but a beast when needed.

My Love,

Things haven't been the same since you're gone
Maybe some people would go to their favorite restaurant
Eat their favorite foods, and enjoy each bite as always

Never again do I want to go where I've gone with you
People would ask about you. I don't want to talk about it
You not being at our favorite places would make them
Into mausoleums of emptiness and loss

In our home, it's like you're still here. I look for you
Daily. I smell your clothes, I lie in your bed, I read your
Poems and I write poems for you. Someday I'll read them to you.

When I Die

I'll visit you
while you're still here.
When you first waken,
you may feel a touch,
like a soft caress,
very much like my hand.

Breakfast passes slowly.
Newspaper doesn't
fill the vacuous silence.
A lone Cheerio
falls gently to the floor.

On the other side
of the quiet table,
no one has eaten Cheerios
since I left,
just one long year ago.

A quiet presence
fills the room.
You are not worried,
for now you know.
Tomorrow will never come.

The Circle

It's a magic circle
This place to walk
This circle in our house

Dining room to kitchen
Kitchen to bedroom
Bedroom to hall
Hall to desk room

Places to collapse
Halfway around
A bed in the bedroom
A cushy leather chair
In the desk room

Not to be deterred
By buckling legs
Or spinning head
Or breath so hard to take

I trudge forward
Around my circle
As if my life were at stake.

Pat Beckemeyer, who lives in Wichita, Kansas, was introduced to poetry at the age of 16 when her high school sweetheart, now her husband Roy, sent her love poems every day at school via his sister. She was drawn more seriously to poetry 10 years ago by a desire to spend more time with her husband. Other than poetry, she is also excited by gardening, bird watching, acrylic painting, butterflies, storms, mountains, oceans and her current Labrador Retriever, Jenna, who appears in several poems.

www.ingramcontent.com/pod-product-compliance
Lightning Source LLC
Chambersburg PA
CBHW030133100526
44591CB00009B/630